The Snail

by Emily Hughes

chronicle books · san francisco

Artists must create
"order out of chaos, a myth out
of the world, a sense of belonging
out of our loneliness."

—Isamu Noguchi

Part 1: Out

An old man shouted into the telephone.

America never wanted me!

Would he like to represent America
in an important exhibition?

The whole world would see it.

No!

The old man was named Isamu.

Isamu was American;
Isamu was Japanese.
Isamu was an artist.

As an artist, he wanted to give gifts to the world.

He wanted to build beautiful
playscapes for children.

America said no.

He wanted to build peace memorials
burning underground.

Japan, too, said no.

So did Isamu feel American?

No.

Did Isamu feel Japanese?

No.

Isamu felt like a snail
and called himself one.

The Snail had been everywhere.

To Tula,

Wahiawā,

Jaipur,

even Gifu, where the cormorants fish.

He had homes in both
New York City, USA,

and Mure, Japan.

But he lived in his shell.
There, the Snail created wonders.

He split, carved, and fought powerful stones.
He called them "bones of the earth,"
so strong they could live forever.

He carefully shaped miniature swing sets,
theater stages, and pottery
so delicate they could break in one drop.

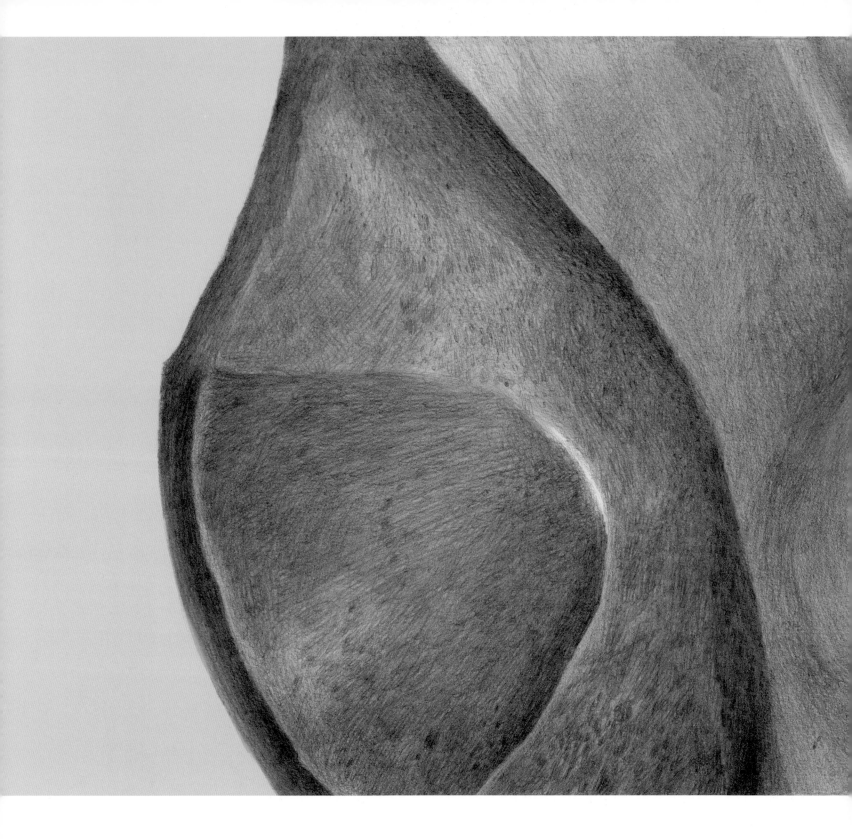

To Isamu they were all sculpture.

He wanted them to be accepted
the way he wished for himself.

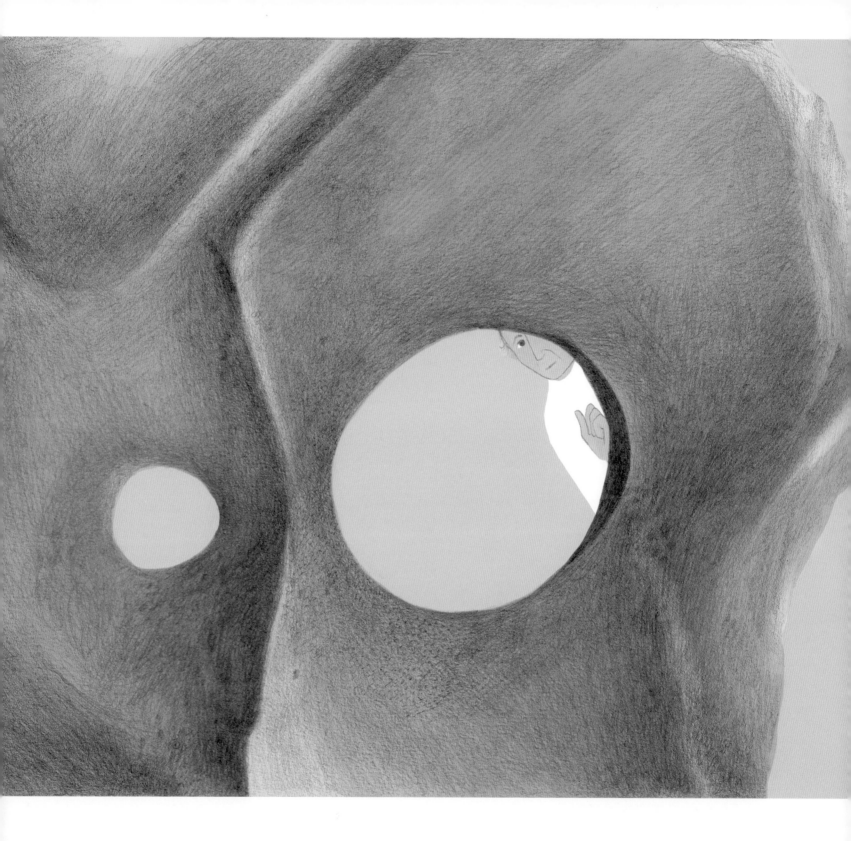

The telephone call only reminded
him of his loneliness.

It made him angry.

He felt it in his body, in his hands.
That would not do.

He looked around the room
and saw akari floating overhead.

While his stones were polished so fine
they reflected the light of the sun,

akari were sculptures that held light within.

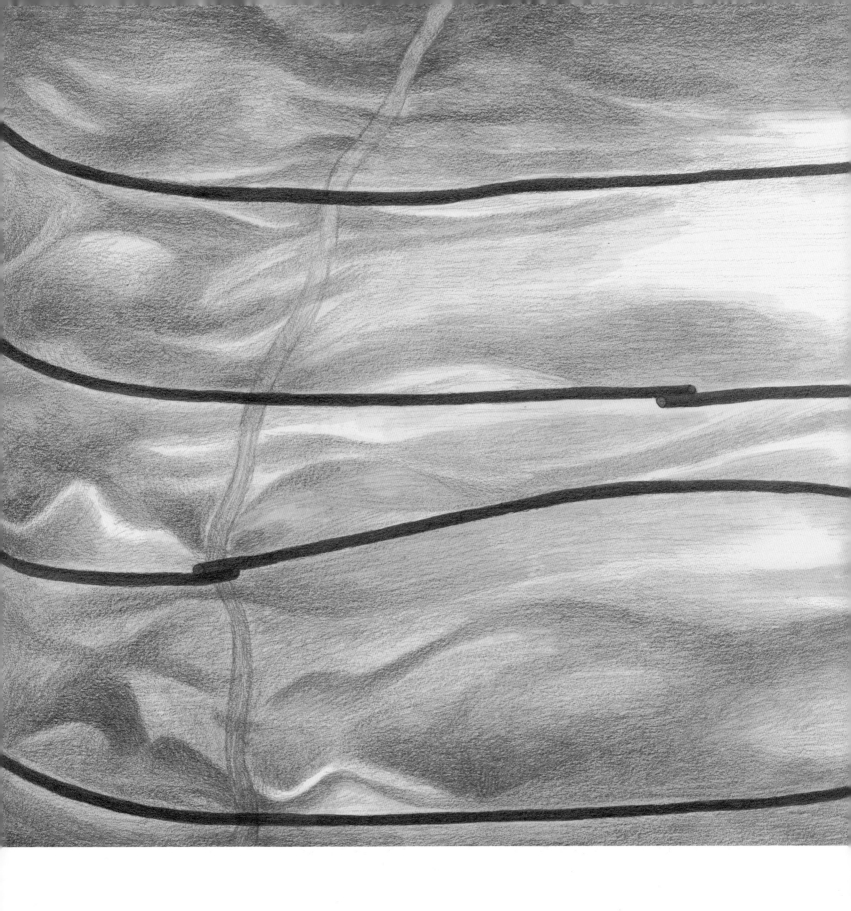

To Isamu

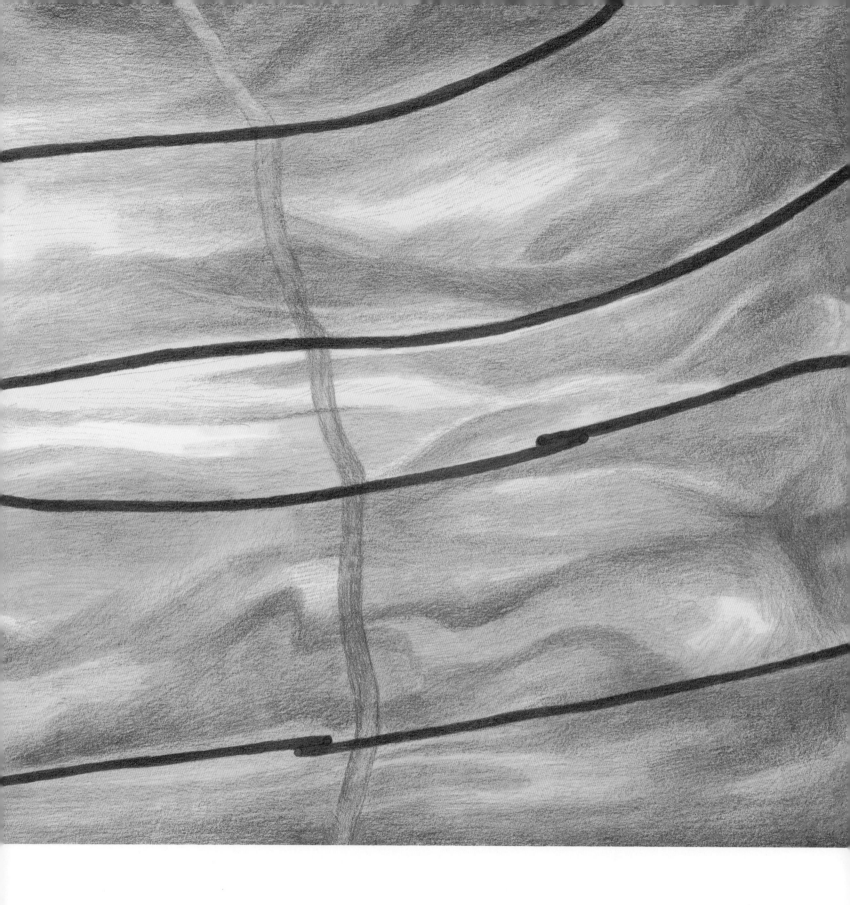

that light was pure gold.

He would build an akari.
Isamu collected his tools

and stepped into his shell.

Part 2: In

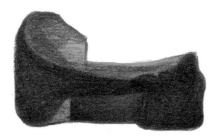

In the shell, Isamu was safe with his memories and dreams and worked with complete focus.

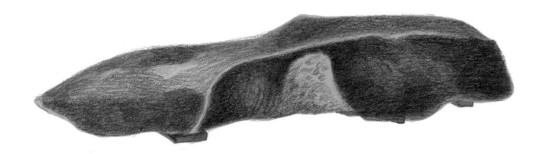

His hands worked so fiercely that those who watched called him

a "typhoon,"   an "ant,"   a "demon."

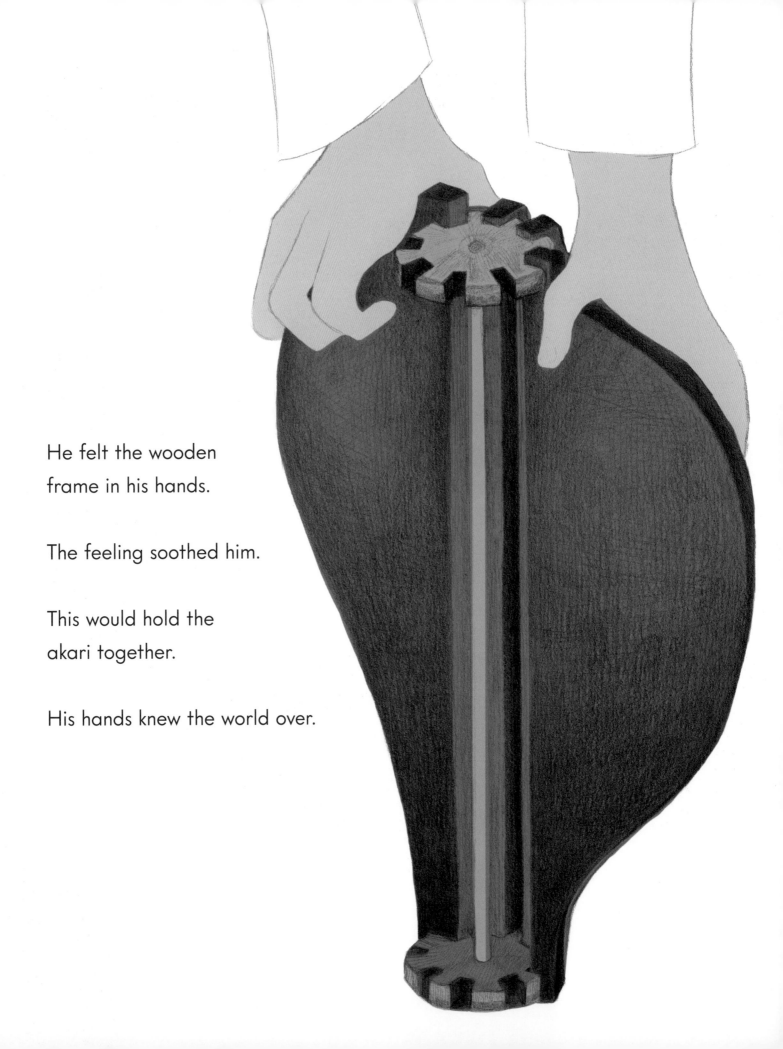

He felt the wooden
frame in his hands.

The feeling soothed him.

This would hold the
akari together.

His hands knew the world over.

They knew the dry soil of the American Southwest

and the rubble of Hiroshima.

A time ago

they had known fear as he turned on
the radio, to the sound of
terrible news.

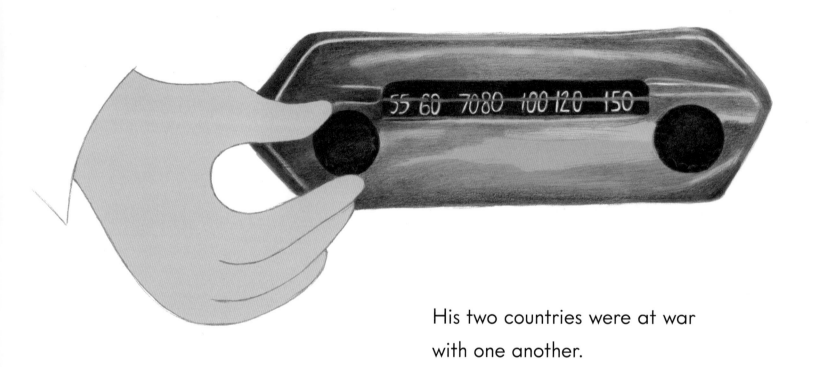

His two countries were at war
with one another.

Who was he to his countries now?

An enemy.

He traveled to Poston, Arizona.
Japanese Americans were relocated there.

Isamu joined them.
He wanted to create beauty and community.

But Poston was not a refuge.
It was a concentration camp.

Isamu left.
The others could not.

When Isamu later saw what
happened to Hiroshima
in the war

he felt neither American
nor Japanese.

He felt ashamed.

He resolved then to be an artist only.

On the frame, the Snail tied a knot with string.

Tiny and hard
like one in your stomach.

Like one in Isamu's stomach a long
time ago.

He was leaving his home, Japan.

Headed to America,
where he had been born

but could not remember.

Isamu's father
demanded that he stay.

Isamu's mother
urged him to go.

In America, he would have
the chance to be himself,

to be an artist.

Isamu looked at his father, Japanese.

Isamu looked at his mother, American.

And chose the lonely journey.

The ropes were cut.

In his shell,
he picked up the thin bamboo,
wrapping it in spirals.

The bamboo curled as Isamu's hair had.
A long, long time ago, when he still had some.

The hair was cursed.
It made him different.

The children called him "gaijin,"

foreigner.

There in Japan, he cut his hair
short.

Later in America, he cut his name
Sam.

No trim, no cut, no change could bring him closer to others.

The Snail turned
the akari's frame.

From
above
it looked
like a fern,

a zenmai.

Zenmai
grew tall
in the shade.

Isamu would walk amongst them to his garden,
a long, long,
long time ago as a boy in Japan.

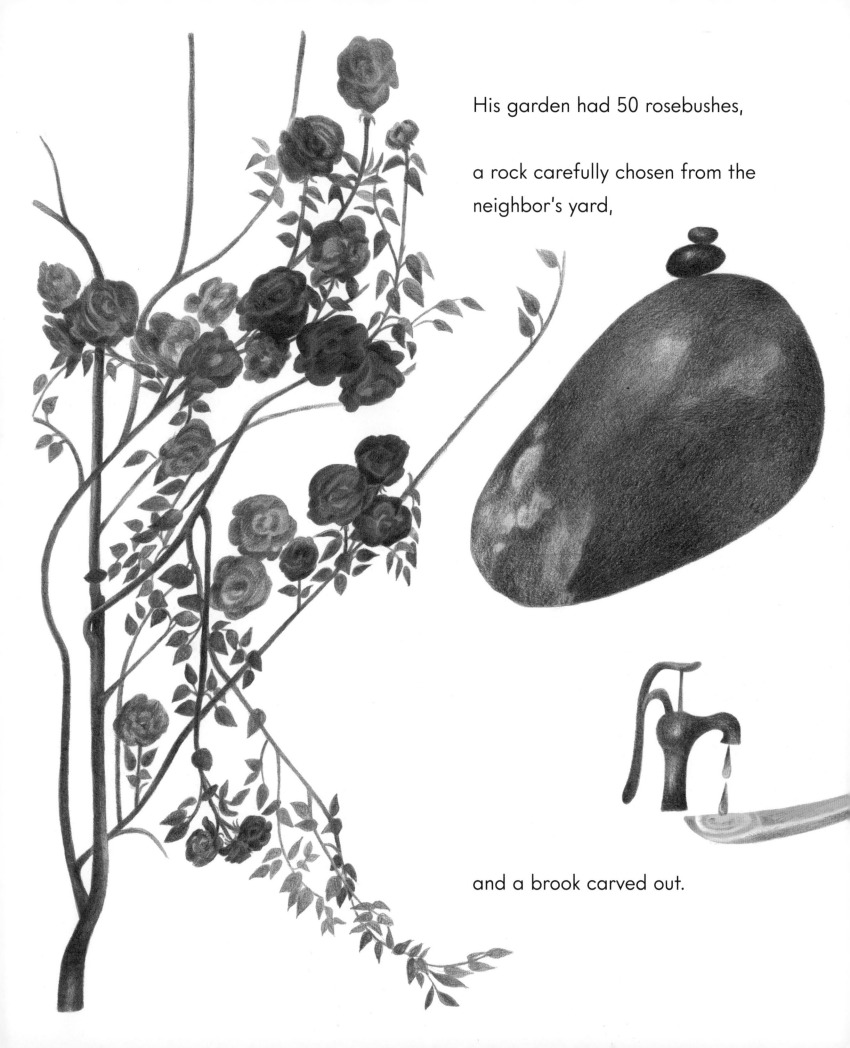

His garden had 50 rosebushes,

a rock carefully chosen from the neighbor's yard,

and a brook carved out.

There alone, the Snail was safe.

The only place he belonged
he had created.

The Snail found himself
deep in his shell.

He breathed in.

He breathed out.

The paper followed.

In.

Out.

Gently, the Snail brushed glue
to the frame and placed the
paper down.

This paper unlike any other.

Paper soft.

Soft as the worn pages of his favorite myths.

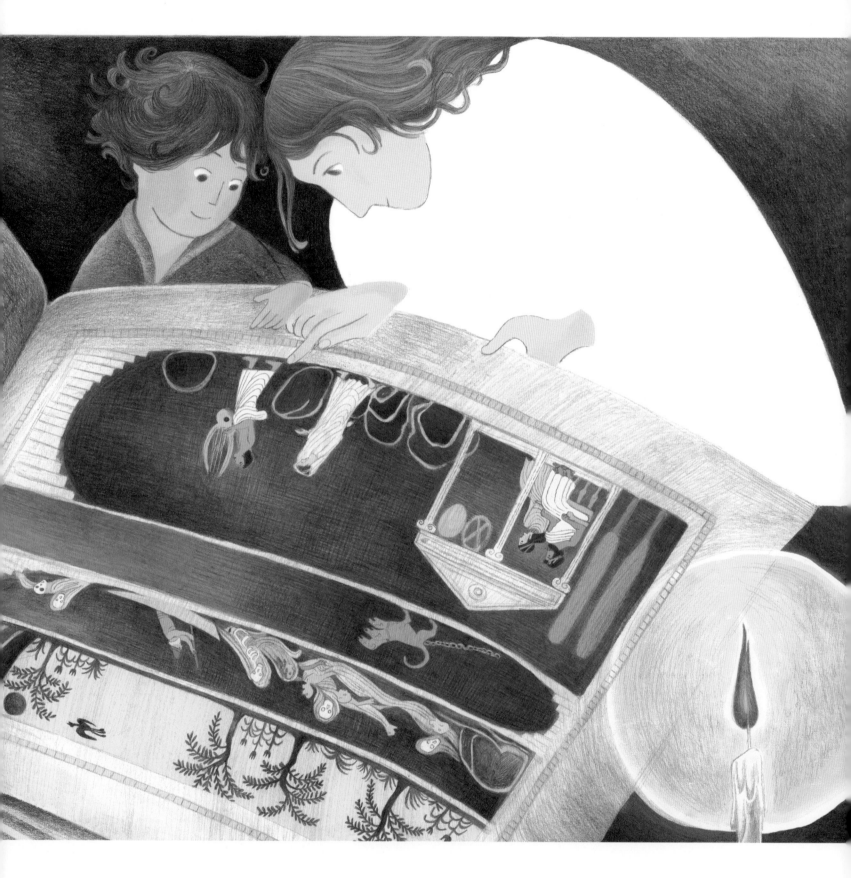

From it he could nearly hear his mother's voice.

Paper comforting

like the light through the shoji door

that soothed a homesick Isamu to sleep.

Paper delicate
like the tent that was his first home.

Held tight and warm within the light of the moon.
A barefoot baby under the California sky.

Part 3: Out Again

Isamu brushed the final sheet down.

The akari shone.

Luminescent

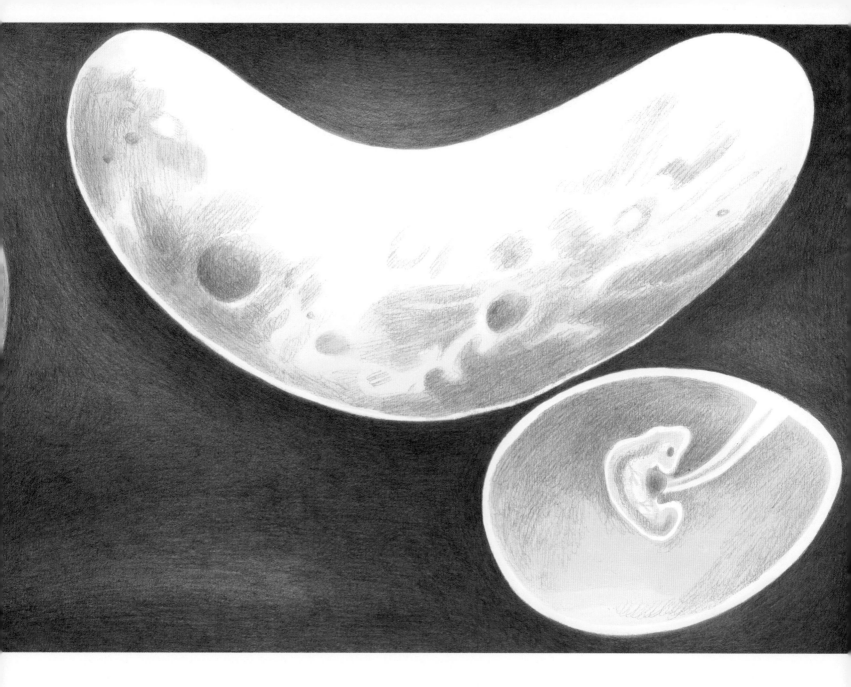

like the sun,   the moon,   an egg.

Isamu had gone into his shell

and walked out the spiral again. He was not as he was before.

He felt love
from the akari's glow.

Neither art nor design,

neither American
nor Japanese.

A marvel all its own.

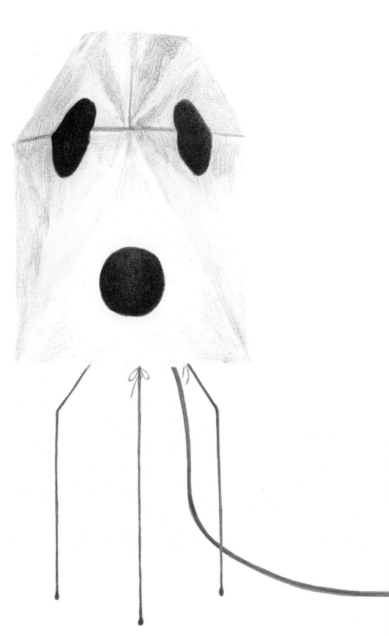

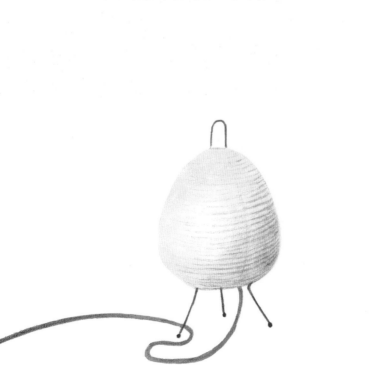

He put the akari in a chest to dry.

He washed his hands
and made a phone call.

Yes.

He would do the exhibition.
And do you know what he made?

A room

full of light.

And a little slide too!

Author's Note

When Isamu Noguchi was asked to participate in the 1986 Venice Biennale, he knew it would be his last hurrah. He was 81 years old.

He initially said no. The memory of Japanese people's treatment in concentration camps still delivered him pain. However, this was his long-awaited chance to be formally accepted and celebrated as an American. After a lifetime of this country thwarting his dreams—basic, professional, even romantic—he still accepted. Saying yes to represent America was brave. He was filled with hope, as all courageous ones are.

The biennale was not a success for Isamu.

His *Slide Mantra* and stone sculptures were received well, but his insistence to keep akari in the show lost him the prize. Critics argued they were too commercial, pushing design over art.

To me, they misunderstood. Akari are sculptures of joy. Sculptures of lightness, impermanence. So unlike those praised at the biennale.

It is a sculpture you can plug into your house's electrical sockets; some would call it a lamp. You can find resemblance in ones a lot cheaper, and ones a lot older, lit by candles.

As Isamu said, "Call it sculpture when it moves you so."

Saying that, Isamu changed the way I viewed everything.

In humble things, I practice viewing. A rock by the side of the road is art. It is a very Japanese idea, but Isamu spread it to the world. Despite his frustrations, he reached through time and did that for me, for anyone who looks at his work.

When I wake in my bedroom far from my family, I am sometimes filled with a sadness that comes in the dark.

It is the familiar light of akari that tends to me.

I am not alone. Beauty is all around me.

When Isamu made akari, he gave us a gift of love.

Bibliography

Apostolos-Cappadona, Diane, and Bruce Altshuler, eds. *Isamu Noguchi: Essays and Conversations*. New York: Harry N. Abrams, 1994.

Ashton, Dore. *Noguchi East and West*. Berkeley: University of California Press, 1992.

Duus, Masayo. *The Life of Isamu Noguchi: Journey without Borders*. Princeton, NJ: Princeton University Press, 2004.

Herrera, Hayden. *Listening to Stone: The Art and Life of Isamu Noguchi*. London: Thames and Hudson, 2015.

Noguchi, Isamu. *Isamu Noguchi: A Sculptor's World*. 1968. Reprint, Göttingen, Germany: Steidl, 2004.